SPIRITUAL GLEANINGS FROM EVERYDAY LIFE

INCIDENTS WITH A SPIRITUAL APPLICATION

Lloyd D. Grimm, Jr.

Author of
A Cup of Cold Water
Called to be a Pastor
Great is Thy Faithfulness
I Will Arise
Sixty-six Days, Sixty-six Books

SCHMUL PUBLISHING COMPANY
NICHOLASVILLE, KENTUCKY

Cover image copyright: <a href="https://www.123rf.com/profile_turbodesign">turbodesign / 123RF Stock Photo</a>. Used by permission.

Cover image copyright: <a href="https://www.123rf.com/profile_artmim">artmim / 123RF Stock Photo</a>Used by permission.

Published by Schmul Publishing Co.
PO Box 776
Nicholasville, KY 40340
USA

Printed in the United States of America

ISBN 10: 0-88019-627-0
ISBN 13: 978-0-88019-627-7

Visit us on the Internet at www.wesleyanbooks.com, or order direct from the publisher by calling 800-772-6657, or by writing to the above address.

Contents

Foreword

FROM READING THE GOSPELS, one readily observes how our Saviour used everyday experiences in order to teach great fundamental spiritual truths. For instance, Jesus taught God's willingness to forgive as he spoke of that lost coin, the lost sheep, and the lost prodigal son (see Luke 15). Many other examples could be cited of the Master converting common life events into constructive spiritual lessons for the benefit and needs of the multitudes. By being alert, we can follow our Lord's strategy in order to meet the spiritual needs of those whom God has placed within the sphere of our influence and responsibility.

Having lived for over four score and ten years, I have experienced many things which have been instrumental in leading me to deep spiritual truth in my walk with God.

The following events are not arranged in any chronological or identical order, but each conveys a spiritual truth, which the author trusts will be of help and encouragement to those who desire a deeper and closer spiritual experience in our Lord and Savior Jesus Christ.

—LLOYD D. GRIMM, JR.

1
Looking Beyond the Filth

"For when we were yet without strength, in due time Christ died for the ungodly. For scarcely for a righteous man will one die: yet peradventure for a good man some would even dare to die. But God commendeth his love toward us, in that, while we were yet sinners, Christ died for us" (Romans 5:6-8).

IT HAS OFTEN BEEN SAID that salvation is free, and that is true if properly understood; for the Word of God says, "Ho, every one that thirsteth, come ye to the waters, and he that hath no money; come ye, buy, and eat; yea, come, buy wine and milk without money and without price" (Isaiah 55:1). It is true our redemption is free in the sense that while we are incapable of meeting the demands of justice, God planned a way to bring broken humanity back into the fold, free of charge to the recipient, but an awful cost to the Donor.

The high cost of God purchasing us back to himself involved a temporary fracture in the Godhead. Through all eternity the Father, Son and Holy Spirit had only known unity. When Jesus died on the cross, He provisionally provided salvation for all mankind, but actually for those who would accept the free gift. In order to do this, our blessed Saviour had to accept the combined suffering of the death of every human being. The very essence of hell is separation from God. For a while on the cross, Jesus tasted death and cried out, "My God, my God, why hast thou forsaken me?" (Matthew 27:46b)

Our scripture mentions the reluctance of one dying for a righteous man, but Jesus went far beyond the thought of giving one's life for a good man, and even prayed for those soldiers as they nailed him to a cruel cross.

God, our dear heavenly Father, so loved us that he was willing to suffer the agony of seeing Jesus on the cross. I have two sons. If one of them were facing crucifixion, I would not hesitate to die in his place. Would not God likewise suffer in the death of his only begotten son? But in order to complete the plan of salvation, it was necessary for the whole Triune Godhead to suffer.

Why did God go so far in order to reconcile a lost guilty world? He looked beyond our guilt, filth and rebellion, and saw what we could become as a result of accepting his plan of salvation.

Some years ago, I was talking to a veteran car salesman. He said he could take a ride in a car and as a result know the condition of the car. Also, when inspecting a car, he would look beyond the dirt. Really, the salesman said he envisioned how the car would look after he worked on it.

In the course of my ministry, I have seen the change of many after they met Jesus Christ. We cannot change the sin of the heart. "Can the Ethiopian change his skin, or the leopard his spots?" (Jeremiah 13:23a) This would be impossible according to nature, but not in the realm of grace. "The things which are impossible with men are possible with God" (Luke 18:27b).

"Come now, and let us reason together, saith the Lord: though your sins be as scarlet, they shall be as white as snow; though they be red like crimson, they shall be as wool" (Isaiah 1:18).

2
Grounded in the Word of God

"Jesus answered and said unto them, Ye do err, not knowing the scriptures, nor the power of God" (Matthew 22:29).

"Thy word have I hid in mine heart, that I might not sin against thee" (Psalm 119:11).

THE FULL ACCOUNT of Jesus' encounter with the Sadducees, from which the above text was taken, is found in Matthew 22:23-32. In this setting, we find these misguided people attempting to disrupt our Lord's ministry by bringing to his attention what they thought would be a case without an answer. They resorted to a law found in Deuteronomy 25:5 where it is stated, "If brethren dwell together, and one of them die, and have no child, the wife of the dead shall not marry without unto a stranger: her husband's brother shall go in unto her, and take her to him to wife, and perform the duty of an husband's brother unto her." Then they used what appears as hyperbole where a point is exaggerated, but should not be taken literally.

Briefly stated, the Sadducees said there was a woman who had seven husbands one at a time, but she outlived them all. Then they asked the master, "Therefore in the resurrection whose wife shall she be of the seven? for they all had her" (Matthew 22:28). Then came Jesus' answer, "Ye do err, not knowing the scriptures, nor the power of God" (Matthew 22:29b).

The Sadducees were the modernists of their day. They did not believe in the resurrection and they were trying to prove Christ's assertion false as our Saviour assures us, "I am the resurrection, and the life: he that believeth in me, though he were dead, yet shall he live: And whosoever liveth and believeth in me shall never die" (John 11:25b-26a).

The only scriptures Sadducees believed were divine was the Pentateuch, which consisted of the first five books of the Bible by Moses. Therefore, our Saviour quotes from the portion of God's Word they accepted. Jesus is telling them they don't know the scripture they accept.

From that vantage point, Jesus goes to the Word of God they accepted as sacred and proved the certainty of life after death. He cites the experience of God speaking to Moses as found in Exodus 3:6a. Jesus answered the Sadducees by saying, "But as touching the resurrection of the dead, have ye not read that which was spoken unto you by God, saying, I am the God of Abraham, and the God of Isaac, and the God of Jacob? God is not the God of the dead, but of the living" (Matthew 22:31-32). At this time Abraham had been physically dead for hundreds of years and God told Moses, I *am still* Abraham's God. He didn't say I *was* his God, but Jesus was inferring that his friend Abraham was still very much alive.

Our Lord and Savior sets an example as to the use of scripture in our daily walk with God. Jesus confronted

Satan by quoting the Word of God. The Apostle Paul mentions the Word of God as a part of our armor in our spiritual warfare, "And take the helmet of salvation, and the sword of the Spirit, which is the Word of God" (Ephesians 6:17).

As God's people, how much time do we spend in absorbing the Word of God until we can recall it in time of need?

I was fortunate to have a pastor in my youth, who became a mentor to me in many areas. One example I followed was his reading the Bible through each year. Thus, I have read the Bible from cover to cover sixty-some times. Although I am now at an advanced age, I still follow that practice.

We need to know the Word for many reasons, but one is in order to detect error and know sound doctrine. From time to time, I hear people quote for scripture what are sayings of men.

Years ago, I had an aunt who taught a Sunday school class. A certain lady spoke up and said, "You know that scripture that says all roads lead to Rome?" Anyone who has knowledge of the Bible will instantly discard that statement as not scripture.

"Thy word is a lamp unto my feet, and a light unto my path" (Psalm 119:105).

3
Appearance can Deceive

"[F]or man looketh on the outward appearance, but the Lord looketh on the heart" (I Samuel 16:7b).

IN ONE OF THE churches I pastored, a man attended who had a supervisory position in a well-known bakery. He told how the company changed the wrapper on their bread with no change of the content. Then, he proceeded to relate how a customer mentioned how good the bread was after the wrapper change.

This incident surely indicates how one can be deceived by outward appearance. When Israel was searching for a king to replace King Saul, the temptation was to make the outward appearance the criteria for their choice. From reading the account, it appears David had brothers who looked more like candidates to head a nation than the young shepherd tending sheep, "But the Lord said unto Samuel, Look not on his countenance, or on the height of his stature; because I have refused him: for the Lord seeth not as man seeth; for man looketh on the outward appearance, but the Lord looketh on the heart" (I Samuel 16:7).

Our Lord Jesus Christ applied this truth to the scribes and Pharisees when he said, "Woe unto you, scribes and Pharisees, hypocrites! for ye are like unto whited sepulchres, which indeed appear beautiful outward, but are within full of dead men's bones, and of all uncleanness" (Matthew 23:27).

These sepulchres looked so clean, but once opened, one finds nothing but decay and stench. So it is with the one untouched by the master. God's Word says, "The heart is deceitful above all things, and desperately wicked: who can know it?" (Jeremiah 17:9) Jesus says, "For out of the heart proceed evil thoughts, murders, adulteries, fornications, thefts, false witness, blasphemies: These are the things which defile a man" (Matthew 15:19-20a).

Choices made from outward appearances can be devastating in all walks of life. The banker who hires one merely because she is young and beautiful and fails to consider the integrity of the prospect may end up with a case of embezzlement. In finding one's mate for life, the same mistake is made many times. A deformed soul is often lodged in a beautiful body. In Proverbs 31:30 we read, "Favour is deceitful, and beauty is vain: but a woman that feareth the Lord, she shall be praised." In the prophecy of Isaiah we read of our dear Lord and Savior Jesus Christ, "For he shall grow up before him as a tender plant, and as a root out of a dry ground: he hath no form nor comeliness; and when we shall see him, there is no beauty that we should desire him" (Isaiah 53:2). While Jesus had no physical beauty according to the verse just quoted, let us read the rest of the chapter and see the sacrifice Jesus Christ made in order that we may partake of his inward beauty, which is all that really matters. For outward beauty fades as the flower, but inner beauty will last through eternity.

"For all that is in the world, the lust of the flesh, and the lust of the eyes, and the pride of life, is not of the Father, but is of the world. And the world passeth away, and the lust thereof: but he that doeth the will of God abideth for ever" (I John 2:16-17).

4
Drawn to Christ or Self?

"Now when they saw the boldness of Peter and John, and perceived that they were unlearned and ignorant men, they marvelled; and they took knowledge of them, that they had been with Jesus" (Acts 4:13).

"And I, if I be lifted up from the earth, will draw all men unto me" (John 12:32).

THE ABOVE ACCOUNT taken from The Acts of the Apostles refers to the time when Peter and John were being questioned by the religious antagonists, because they were "grieved that they taught the people, and preached through Jesus the resurrection from the dead" (Acts 4:2b).

Prior to this setting, Jesus told how he would draw all men unto him if he was "lifted up from the earth", or in other words, would die on the cross in order to save mankind from sin. We find this literally taking place after the Apostle Peter, now filled with the Holy Spirit, preached. "Then they that gladly received his word were baptized: and the same day there were added unto them about three thousand souls" (Acts 2:41).

What caused so many to be drawn to the Lord? Was it Peter's sermon? To those who would answer Yes, I ask then, why was he not effective the three years he followed Jesus during our Lord's public ministry?

The only genuine conclusion is this great revival took place in fulfillment of our Saviour's promise that he would draw all men unto him by his death on the cross, and further promised that he would send the Holy Spirit to administer this great plan of salvation. "But ye shall receive power, after that the Holy Ghost is come upon you: and ye shall be witnesses unto me both in Jerusalem, and in all Judaea, and in Samaria, and unto the uttermost part of the earth" (Acts 1:8).

As a result, people were drawn to Jesus Christ and not to the Apostles Peter and John. They didn't forget these now Spirit-filled men, but saw them in the light of a different perspective. Now, they looked at the apostles and saw Jesus' image reflected in them. Those looking on the phenomenon were drawn to our Saviour, resulting in the conversion of "about three thousand souls" (Acts 2:41b).

As I close these thoughts, there are some searching questions all of us need to ponder, whether as laymen or ministers. Is my one goal to draw all men to Jesus or do I have an underlying desire to exalt self? Am I as much interested in witnessing to one who I will never see again as I am in those who are good prospects for my particular church? As pastors, do we use soul winning as a means of building a reputation in order to receive a so-called promotion?

So, do our lives draw people to Christ or to ourselves? Years ago, I was talking to a businessman and in the course of our conversation, he told me of a minister who attracted many. Then suddenly, he said as a matter of fact, "Of course, you would not want him around you if you were dying." The thing that really took hold of me was the sincerity of this individual, for there was no jesting in our conversation. I have no idea as to the identity of this pastor, or to the denomination he was affiliated with. Furthermore, the Word of God warns us of the danger of evil surmise. It is easy to draw conclusions with scant evidence. We are not to judge (see Matthew 7:1); nevertheless, the world is reading our lives.

In John 9:5 Jesus said, "As long as I am in the world, I am the light of the world." We read in Matthew 5:14a, "Ye are the light of the world." How do we reconcile these scriptures? Briefly stated, we are to continue Christ's ministry, by the anointing of the Holy Spirit. As the moon reflects the light of the sun, we will reflect Jesus in our lives and souls will be drawn to Christ and not to us.

In those early days, men could not help but see Jesus as they met the Spirit-filled disciples and were drawn to him. The good news is that this can happen and will take place in these modern times if we tarry for the baptism of the Holy Spirit and fire (see Matthew 3:11).

Last words are treasured and appear as a summary of a man's life. Some of the last words of our Saviour were, "And, behold, I send the promise of my Father upon you: but tarry ye in the city of Jerusalem, until ye be endued with power from on high" (Luke 24:49).

When this experience takes place, those looking on will naturally be drawn to Jesus and not to us.

5
Strength for the Day

"If thou hast run with the footmen, and they have wearied thee, then how canst thou contend with horses? and if in the land of peace, wherein thou trustedst, they wearied thee, then how wilt thou do in the swelling of Jordan?" (Jeremiah 12:5)

"Behold, he shall come up like a lion from the swelling of Jordan" (Jeremiah 49:19a).

"[A]nd as thy days, so shall thy strength be" (Deuteronomy 33:25b).

THE PROPHET JEREMIAH WAS truly a man of God, but he still had a problem, that if left unattended could eventually destroy his faith. This puzzle is still confusing in these modern days until we prayerfully study the Word of God. Then, what is the perplexity? Briefly stated it is, Why do the righteous suffer out of proportion to the wicked?

The psalmist faced this dilemma as recorded in Psalm 73, which should be read in its entirety. A portion reads,

"Truly God is good to Israel, even to such as are of a clean heart. But as for me, my feet were almost gone; my steps had well nigh slipped. For I was envious at the foolish, when I saw the prosperity of the wicked" (Psalm 73:1-3). Then after describing what he observed, he found the answer, like King Hezekiah who turned it all over to God. We read, "When I thought to know this, it was too painful for me; Until I went into the sanctuary of God; then understood I their end" (Psalm 73:16-17).

This inspired writer, who was mightily used of God to deliver the message of this Psalm, had nearly backslid when he looked at people instead of focusing his vision on God. In one of the churches I served as pastor, a lady failed in her walk with God many times and became a chronic seeker as she looked at human beings, when this sister should have heeded the Word of God, "Looking unto Jesus the author and finisher of our faith" (Hebrews 12:2a).

The Prophet Habakkuk had the same temptation as the Psalmist had, but as he sought God he worked his way through all doubt, and left an inspiring testimony of encouragement to all generations. It reads, "Although the fig tree shall not blossom, neither shall fruit be in the vines; the labour of the olive shall fail, and the fields shall yield no meat; the flock shall be cut off from the fold, and there shall be no herd in the stalls: Yet I will rejoice in the Lord, I will joy in the God of my salvation. The Lord God is my strength, and he will make my feet like hinds' feet, and he will make me to walk upon mine high places" (Habakkuk 3:17-19a).

With these thoughts in mind, let us return to Jeremiah's problem and God's answer. It is worthy to note the prophet's approach to God as he casts his burden on his Creator. It is with deep respect, reverence and humility that he dares to reason with the Almighty concerning what He permits and His dealing with humankind. Let us notice how Jeremiah begins his appeal. "Righteous art thou, O Lord, when I plead with thee: yet let me talk with thee of thy judgments: Wherefore doth the way of the wicked prosper? wherefore are all they happy that deal very treacherously? (Jeremiah 12:1) The prophet is certain that God's judgments are right, but with his finite mind he fails to understand. God didn't give Jeremiah a direct answer, but intimates that things were going to get worse. If he could not stand when things were relatively peaceful, "What will you do in the swelling of Jordan?" When the River Jordan caused a flood, it drove the lions and other beasts of prey out and into the country where they took the lives of men and carried their cattle away.

God is weaning Jeremiah away from trusting for more favorable circumstances in order to live a God-fearing victorious life, so the prophet will find God is the ultimate source of strength regardless of the fierce storms we face in this life.

Later in this chapter, our Lord tells Jeremiah about the more difficult battles of faith that he will experience. How would you feel or how would I feel after praying for help concerning severe temptations, only to get an answer that the worst is yet to come? I was just a boy, but I still remember our pastor placing a poem in front of the church for all to read:

"From the time you are born
until you ride in a hearse
things have never been so bad
but what they could have been worse."

I was young and that may have contributed to my slowness and grasping the saying, for I read the word "hearse" as "horse." However, there is truth in the saying. I had an aunt who said, in effect, "All you need to solve a problem is to get a bigger one." Of course, a more complex problem will not dispel the original, but it temporarily relieves the mind.

But God has a purpose in allowing us to be tried and tested. Satan's plan in temptations is to destroy and turn us against God. The Apostle Peter warns us, "Be sober, be vigilant; because your adversary the devil, as a roaring lion, walketh about, seeking whom he may devour: Whom resist stedfast in the faith, knowing that the same afflictions are accomplished in your brethren that are in the world" (I Peter 5:8-9).

But God's purpose in times of testing is to increase our spiritual stamina. We see examples of this truth in the lives of Abraham, Job, and many others who have volunteered to enlist in the army of the Lord.

When we give ourselves unconditionally to the Lord, and are filled with the Holy Spirit, we will soon find the reality of spiritual warfare that St. Paul mentions in Ephesians 6:10-20. "Put on the whole armour of God, that ye may be able to stand against the wiles of the devil. For we wrestle not against flesh and blood, but against principalities, against powers, against the rulers of the darkness of this world, against spiritual wickedness in high places" (Ephesians 6:11-12).

In these battles, God's design is to increase our strength and prepare us for greater service in the building of the Kingdom. Paul prayed three times for the removal of what he called "a thorn in the flesh" (see II Corinthians 12:7). Although he was not healed, Jesus answered, "My grace is sufficient for thee: for my strength is made perfect in weakness" (part of II Corinthians 12:9).

So, it is not how huge our battle, but the strength of the true and living God we serve. God's reassuring words to Joshua as he assumed the leadership of God's people apply to all who serve him. "Have not I commanded thee?

Be strong and of a good courage; be not afraid, neither be thou dismayed: for the Lord thy God is with thee whithersoever thou goest" (Joshua 1:9).

6
Promotion as God Views It

"Jesus knowing that the Father had given all things into his hands, and that he was come from God, and went to God; He riseth from supper, and laid aside his garments; and took a towel, and girded himself. After that he poureth water into a bason, and began to wash the disciples' feet, and to wipe them with the towel wherewith he was girded" (John 13:3-5).

PRIOR TO PENTECOST THERE WAS rivalry among the disciples as to who was the greatest. Even John and his brother James were interested in having the chief seats in Christ's kingdom (see Matthew 20:20-28). Here Jesus made it clear not only to his disciples, but to all, that the way for promotion is not to make that a goal, but humble, lowly service will naturally result in unsolicited promotion. Jesus said, "[W]hosoever will be chief among you, let him be your servant: Even as the Son of man came not to be ministered unto, but to minister, and to give his life a ransom for many" (Matthew 20:27-28).

Who is this that takes the place of a slave and humbly begins to wash the feet of his disciples? Newcomers looking on at first glance would probably say, Just another slave at work, but then they notice a difference from what they commonly see in this ritual. This slave goes about his work in such a tender, loving way. Has he been trained to work for those in high authority? What are his credentials?

For an answer to this question, we must resort to the scriptures. "All things were made by him; and without him was not any thing made that was made. In him was life; and the life was the light of men" (John 1:3-4). Here is the one who created the universe condescending to do the work of the slave, and that which was reserved as the duty of the lowest slaves. Jesus left all the riches and glory of heaven so we can enjoy his joy through all eternity if we accept him. The inspired Apostle Paul writes, "For ye know the grace of our Lord Jesus Christ, that, though he was rich, yet for your sakes he became poor, that ye through his poverty might be rich" (II Corinthians 8:9).

In the light of this act of humility performed by our Saviour, "leaving us an example, that ye should follow his steps" (I Peter 2:21b), what should be our response? What do you think? If Christ gave up all his riches in heaven to make us rich in all spiritual life and blessing, can we do less than lay aside all carnal desire for promotion, and desire to be promoted only if it will result in being equipped better to serve God in the building of his Kingdom?

God does not call us to fail, and in one way or another promotion will come, for God's people follow his Word as it applies to their work. In the Book of Romans and in many other scriptures, we find a follower of Christ cannot be lazy. "Not slothful in business; fervent in spirit; serving the Lord" (Romans 12:11). As we daily practice the teaching of God's Word, we will become better workers, whatever occupation, profession or calling we follow, the result being a tendency for promotion.

In the meanwhile, we will be content where God has placed us regardless of the hardships involved. As a young pastor I served a very small church that had serious problems. I called on an older evangelist who like Barnabas was a good man, "For he was a good man and full of the Holy Ghost and of faith" (Acts 11:24a). This saintly man of God made a statement to me that made an indelible impression on my mind. He said, "It is better to be a big man in a little place than to be a little man in a big place."

Just stop and think how the truth of this quotation can be applied in the entire course of our Saviour's ministry. In the prophecy of Isaiah we read, "Thus saith God the Lord, he that created the heavens, and stretched them out; he that spread forth the earth, and that which cometh out of it; he that giveth breath unto the people upon it, and spirit to them that walk therein" (Isaiah 42:5). This is the one described by the prophet, who is the true and living God, who takes the place of the lowest slave and washes the feet of his disciples. Should not all selfish desire for promotion blush and give way in the light of this account?

"And whosoever will be chief among you, let him be your servant" (Matthew 20:27).

7

"By All Means Save Some"

(I Corinthians 9:22b)

"Now while Paul waited for them at Athens, his spirit was stirred in him, when he saw the city wholly given to idolatry. Therefore disputed he in the synagogue with the Jews, and with the devout persons, and in the market daily with them that met with him. Then certain philosophers of the Epicureans, and of the Stoicks, encountered him. And some said, What will this babbler say? other some, He seemeth to be a setter forth of strange gods: because he preached unto them Jesus, and the resurrection. And they took him, and brought him unto Areopagus, saying, May we know what this new doctrine, whereof thou speakest, is? For thou bringest certain strange things to our ears: we would know therefore what these things mean. (For all the Athenians and strangers which were there spent their time in nothing else, but either to tell, or to hear some new thing.) Then Paul stood in the midst of Mars' hill, and said, Ye men of Athens, I perceive that in all things ye are too superstitious.

For as I passed by, and beheld your devotions, I found an altar with this inscription, TO THE UNKNOWN GOD. Whom therefore ye ignorantly worship, him declare I unto you" (Acts 17:16-23).

The Apostle Paul took advantage of every opportunity in order to bring the lost to Jesus Christ. He made use of his spare time. While Paul was waiting for Silas and Timothy to join him at Athens, an unexpected door opened for him to preach to an intelligent people, but people who were groping in spiritual darkness, ignorantly seeking for the true and living God.

Here Paul found those who were hungering and thirsting for that which would satisfy the spiritual vacuum they experienced. They had tried every conceivable means to meet this spiritual need. They exhausted their list of gods and in desperation they constructed "an altar with this inscription, TO THE UNKNOWN GOD" (part of Acts 17:23). The modern world today is following the same course by thinking material wealth, pleasure, popularity, etc. will satisfy the spiritual nature of man, but sadly disappointed they will be forced to join Solomon and cry out, "Vanity of vanities... all is vanity" (part of Ecclesiastes 12:8).

The Apostle seized this providential setting in order to lead these folks to a saving knowledge of our Lord Jesus Christ. He had to be very careful in his approach, for the local law prohibited introducing a new religion. So, Paul tactfully agreed to the reality of their one unseen God without compromising the gospel, but was quick to point them to the Living God. (Read the full account in Acts 17:16-34.)

He didn't ridicule their false way of worship, for the fact they were seeking after God, although ignorantly, proved they were seeking truth and responding to the call of the Holy Spirit.

Paul could have alienated their attention to his message by scoffing at their worship of many idols, but he got right to the heart of the matter, and preached Jesus Christ as our only hope in order to be accepted on that Judgment Day (see Acts 17:30-31).

In our day there is much instruction concerning the proper approach to soul winning, but the best proven Textbook is simply God's Word, the Holy Bible.

We could well follow the Apostle's technique as we witness to the lost. I knew a woman who was trying to work her way into heaven. Listen to Ephesians 2:8-9: "For by grace are ye saved through faith; and that not of yourselves: it is the gift of God: Not of works, lest any man should boast."

This kind lady made it a practice to take care of stray animals. She said she did this so she would go to heaven. At first thought this may seem absurd, but it proves the Holy Spirit was dealing with her. If we would follow St. Paul's approach in witnessing, we would commend her for such humane treatment of the lower creation. The soul winner could quote, "A righteous man regardeth the life of his beast" (Proverbs 12:10a). Now, having won her confidence, we could proceed to present the gospel and lead her to Christ.

Even in dealing with fellow Christians and we see something that needs to be corrected, one should be courteous and respect the views of the individual confronted. Apollos was an eloquent man and mighty in the scriptures (see Acts 18:24-28). This man was instructed in the way of the Lord, knowing only the baptism of John. "And he began to speak boldly in the synagogue: whom when Aquila and Priscilla had heard, they took him unto them, and expounded unto him the way of God more perfectly" (Acts 18:26). Apollos must have corrected that which he lacked for the following two verses show that after meeting with

Aquila and Priscilla he went from there and had a powerful ministry.

Even with the best approach delivered by the saintly Apostle Paul, there were those who mocked while some procrastinated and turned a deaf ear to the Gospel. But some believed. I find modern man reacts much in the same way, but one soul is worth much more than the whole world, so let us reach out to a perishing world and "by all means save some" (I Corinthians 9:22b).

8
Intellectual or Spiritual Problem

"For the preaching of the cross is to them that perish foolishness; but unto us which are saved it is the power of God. For it is written, I will destroy the wisdom of the wise, and will bring to nothing the understanding of the prudent. Where is the wise? where is the scribe? where is the disputer of this world? hath not God made foolish the wisdom of this world? For after that in the wisdom of God the world by wisdom knew not God, it pleased God by the foolishness of preaching to save them that believe. For the Jews require a sign, and the Greeks seek after wisdom: But we preach Christ crucified, unto the Jews a stumblingblock, and unto the Greeks foolishness; But unto them which are called, both Jews and Greeks, Christ the power of God, and the wisdom of God" (I Corinthians 1:18-24).

THE KINGDOM OF GOD IS BARRED to those who seek to enter it by the vain philosophies of this world. In verse 22b, we find the Greeks sought wisdom in order to find God, only to fail in their search:

"...the world by wisdom knew not God" (part of I Corinthians 1:21). I think it was Socrates, a Greek philosopher, who was a good, sincere seeker after Truth, but testified only that he almost saw the Light.

The true Light and Way is found only in our Lord Jesus Christ. When Thomas asked the Master the way to heaven, Jesus responded by saying, "I am the way, the truth, and the life: no man cometh unto the Father, but by me" (John 14:6b). Also, we read in John 10:1, "Verily, verily, I say unto you, He that entereth not by the door into the sheepfold, but climbeth up some other way, the same is a thief and a robber." Then in the same discourse Jesus said, "All that ever came before me are thieves and robbers: but the sheep did not hear them. I am the door: by me if any man enter in, he shall be saved, and shall go in and out, and find pasture" (John 10:8-9).

While the Greeks used their wisdom in a search for God, the Jews required a sign or proof before they would believe. The rich man in hell, when he realized there was no release from his sentence, became concerned for his five brothers who were following the same road leading to eternal damnation. He asked Abraham to send Lazarus to testify and warn his brothers of the danger they faced if they continued to reject Jesus Christ as Saviour. "Abraham saith unto him, They have Moses and the prophets; let them hear them" (Luke 16:29). In other words, they had the inspired writings of the Old Testament that shed enough light on their pathway to lead them to heaven. Jesus concluded this message by saying, "If they hear not Moses and the prophets, neither will they be persuaded, though one rose from the dead" (Luke 16:31b).

God's method to reach and bring salvation to a world lost in sin is by the preaching of his inspired word. "For after that in the wisdom of God the world by wisdom knew not God, it pleased God by the foolishness of preaching to save them that believe" (I Corinthians 1:21). Those who rejected Christ and sought for truth by other means thought preaching was foolishness. The word translated "foolishness" means *irrational* or *stupid*. But we who "have tasted the good Word of God, and the powers of the world to come" (Hebrews 6:5b) experience a certainty that is available to all who are fully surrendered to God. The Apostle Paul preached with authority, for God had full possession of him. Listen to the apostle: "But we preach Christ crucified, unto the Jews a stumblingblock, and unto the Greeks foolishness; But unto them which are called, both Jews and Greeks, Christ the power of God, and the wisdom of God" (I Corinthians 1:23-24).

In one of my pastorates, there was a young man in his teens who claimed he had an intellectual problem that kept him from coming to the Lord. Like the rich young ruler who had kept all the commandments but lacked Christ, so this teenager appeared spotless morally. We had one of those services when the Holy Spirit came upon the church in power and "the waters were troubled" (see John 5:1-9). Stanley came to the altar and God met his need and his intellectual problem was resolved. I like the way new Christians, who have not learned the way and language we usually hear in a testimony, express their feelings. He simply said, "I feel like I have been repaired." He was recast. The great Heavenly Potter did for this young man what God wanted to do for Israel. "And the vessel that he made of clay was marred in the hand of the potter: so he made it again another vessel, as seemed good to the potter to make it" (Jeremiah 18:4).

Whatever your problem that seems to block your way to the Saviour, confess it and all sin to Jesus believing, and you will not be disappointed. "For whosoever shall call upon the name of the Lord shall be saved" (Romans 10:13).

9
Home: Castle or Prison?

"Now a certain man was sick, named Lazarus, of Bethany, the town of Mary and her sister Martha. (It was that Mary which anointed the Lord with ointment, and wiped his feet with her hair, whose brother Lazarus was sick.) Therefore his sisters sent unto him, saying, Lord, behold, he whom thou lovest is sick. When Jesus heard that, he said, This sickness is not unto death, but for the glory of God, that the Son of God might be glorified thereby. Now Jesus loved Martha, and her sister, and Lazarus" (John 11:1-5)

"Then Jesus six days before the passover came to Bethany, where Lazarus was, which had been dead, whom he raised from the dead. There they made him a supper; and Martha served: but Lazarus was one of them that sat at the table with him. Then took Mary a pound of ointment of spikenard, very costly, and anointed the feet of Jesus, and wiped his feet with her hair: and the house was filled with the odour of the ointment" (John 12:1-3)

WHEN JESUS TOOK ON him the nature of man, God's Word says, "Wherefore in all things it behoved him to be made like unto his brethren, that he might be a merciful and faithful high priest in things pertaining to God, to make reconciliation for the sins of the people" (Hebrews 2:17). Therefore, by taking on human nature, he naturally loved social gatherings as we see him taking part in the celebration of the marriage in Cana of Galilee.

The home is a social unit, but Jesus had no home. The Saviour said, "The foxes have holes, and the birds of the air have nests; but the Son of man hath not where to lay his head" (Matthew 8:20b). In the Gospel of John 7:53-8:1 we read, "And every man went unto his own house. Jesus went unto the mount of Olives." Was there no one among the crowds that followed Jesus who would give him a night's lodging? This can happen today. This was re-enacted in the earlier ministry of my friend, Dr. R.D. Brown, who is now in heaven where he is amply cared for. He was holding a meeting in a mountain area and evidently provision was not made for his entertainment. This good man's diet at that time consisted of blackberries and spring water he found on the mountain.

However, there were homes where Jesus knew he was welcome. One of them was the home of Mary, Martha and Lazarus. After a day of toil meeting the various needs of the multitudes, we can only imagine the comfort, peace and rest offered by a family united in love for one another and their Saviour.

We all need such a home as a retreat where we are restored and able again to face both the challenges and difficulties that arise in the course of living. But, sad to say, many homes are more like a prison than a retreat or castle.

I heard a speaker tell about a conversation he heard while dining in a restaurant. When the waitress took his order, this unknown man told her that he wanted this to be like home. He told her to burn his toast, then sit across from him and nag him while he ate it. Alas, this pictures many of our homes today.

While this account may appear comical, it is really serious. God planned for our homes to be a happy retreat where the family is united in love serving Him. This happens when all the members of a family serve God. But many of God's children experience the reverse of this ideal.

You may be the only one in your family serving God. Do not despair. God will more than compensate if you are fully surrendered to his will. When Israel was far from their homes, they found a promise from God. In Ezekiel 11:16b we read, "Thus saith the Lord God; Although I have cast them far off among the heathen, and although I have scattered them among the countries, yet will I be to them as a little sanctuary in the countries where they shall come" (Ezekiel 11:16b).

Also, God can change home conditions as the individual members of the family surrender to Christ and are changed. This takes place as God's children reflect the beauty of Jesus in their everyday walk with the Master, but if they reveal traits of carnality it will repulse the sinner from accepting Jesus Christ as Lord and Saviour. In I Peter 3:1 one reads, "Likewise, ye wives, be in subjection to your own husbands; that, if any obey not the word, they also may without the word be won by the conversation of the wives." A revival worker was being entertained in a home where evidently the husband did not attend church. After his wife and the special workers left for the revival, the husband prepared a meal for all. The guests said when they returned, the wife of this man criticized her husband. If she ever expected her husband to find the Lord, she should have shown appreciation for what he did, even if not performed perfectly. In contrast to this incident, I knew an elderly minister, a good Spirit-filled man, who many times filled the pulpit for me in my absence. I think it was when he or his wife went to be with the Lord, their daughter said she had never heard an unkind word between them, or something similar. "Her children arise up, and call her blessed" (Proverbs 31:28a).

May we all strive to make our homes a happy retreat and not a prison. This goal will take place when we are forgiven and filled with the Holy Spirit.

10
The Origin of Sin

"But the tongue can no man tame; it is an unruly evil, full of deadly poison. Therewith bless we God, even the Father; and therewith curse we men, which are made after the similitude of God. Out of the same mouth proceedeth blessing and cursing. My brethren, these things ought not so to be. Doth a fountain send forth at the same place sweet water and bitter? Can the fig tree, my brethren, bear olive berries? either a vine, figs? so can no fountain both yield salt water and fresh" (James 3:8-12).

"But those things which proceed out of the mouth come forth from the heart; and they defile the man. For out of the heart proceed evil thoughts, murders, adulteries, fornications, thefts, false witness, blasphemies: These are the things which defile a man" (Matthew 15:18-20a).

IN THE PROPHECY OF Jeremiah we read, "Can the Ethiopian change his skin, or the leopard his spots? then may ye also do good, that are accustomed to do evil"

(Jeremiah 13:23). In practical everyday experiences this scripture proves what God has declared in Jeremiah 17:9, "The heart is deceitful above all things, and desperately wicked: who can know it?"

All sin springs from a corrupt condition of the uncleansed heart which all have received through the fall of Adam. Men try to heal the problem sin produces without touching the infection. Cleaning up the environment, educating the public, etc., at best is scarcely a Band-Aid to the avalanche of problems sin produces.

The writer has lived a long life, but clearly remembers attending a small country school where one of the students evidently had said something considered sinful. I can still picture the teacher washing that little boy's mouth with soap. He needed a teacher who would have tenderly but firmly pointed him to our Saviour who died to cleanse our hearts from sin.

In ages past and those to come, if God tarries, man will continue to follow such absurd ways to heal the problems of sin. God's Word describes this approach to the problem as "ever learning, and never able to come to the knowledge of the truth" (II Timothy 3:7). There are not many ways, but there is one way, and only one way, that will solve the problem of sin. This living way is found in John 14:6b where Jesus told Thomas, "I am the way, the truth, and the life: no man cometh unto the Father, but by me."

People try desperately to find other ways. Many years ago, a lady told me that she felt her sins would be washed away if only she could get out into the water. In answer to her search, God says, "But if we walk in the light, as he is in the light, we have fellowship one with another, and the blood of Jesus Christ his Son cleanseth us from all sin" (I John 1:7).

The vision the Prophet Isaiah saw concerning Judah and Jerusalem pictures the sinful conditions of all men outside of our Lord and Savior Jesus Christ. "Ah sinful nation, a people laden with iniquity, a seed of evildoers, children that are corrupters: they have forsaken the Lord, they have provoked the Holy One of Israel unto anger, they are gone away backward. Why should ye be stricken any more? ye will revolt more and more: the whole head is sick, and the whole heart faint. From the sole of the foot even unto the head there is no soundness in it; but wounds, and bruises, and putrifying sores: they have not been closed, neither bound up, neither mollified with ointment" (Isaiah 1:4-6).

The Word of God states, "For all have sinned, and come short of the glory of God" (Romans 3:23). Some have gone deeper into the practice of sin, but in the Book of James we read, "For whosoever shall keep the whole law, and yet offend in one point, he is guilty of all" (James 2:10). Therefore, all sin stems from a fallen, corrupt nature we inherited from the fall of Adam.

In his prayer of repentance King David said, "For I acknowledge my transgressions: and my sin is ever before me" (Psalm 51:3). He was miserable and realized he could do nothing to change the past, but the king knew of One who had the power to forgive, change his heart and give him a new start. So, in verse 7 David prayed, "Purge me with hyssop, and I shall be clean: wash me, and I shall be whiter than snow."

Sin is an awful malady of the soul and must not be dealt with lightly, but there is hope for all who confess and repent as David did in Psalm 51. You may feel your sin is too bad for God to forgive. Like David, we can't go back, but we can go forward. One of the greatest saints I've ever met told me that if he had lived in Old Testament times, he would have been put to death for his sin. The same could be said of this man that was said by Jesus of the sinful woman who anointed the feet of our Saviour, "Wherefore I say unto thee, her sins, which are many, are forgiven; for she loved much: but to whom little is forgiven, the same loveth little" (Luke 7:47).

When forgiven and cleansed from sin, we should believe God and not waste valuable time brooding over past failure and sin. I need not know how deep you have sinned, but I can assure you on authority of God's Word, there is forgiveness and cleansing if you heed the Holy Spirit's call. "If we confess our sins, he is faithful and just to forgive us our sins, and to cleanse us from all unrighteousness" (I John 1:9).

11
A Clear Conscience

"And herein do I exercise myself, to have always a conscience void to offence toward God, and toward men" (Acts 24:16).

THE TEXT IS FROM the Apostle Paul's defense and testimony before Felix. He was bound with man-made chains but free with a God-given clean conscience. The authorities could deprive him of his supposed freedom, but not from the genuine freedom that only God's children experience. Jesus says, "If the Son therefore shall make you free, ye shall be free indeed" (John 8:36). This was the freedom Simon Peter had when King Herod was plotting his death. It enabled the Apostle to sleep soundly under such trying circumstances. "And, behold, the angel of the Lord came upon him, and a light shined in the prison: and he smote Peter on the side, and raised him up, saying, Arise up quickly. And his chains fell off from his hands" (Acts 12:7).

All men are capable of experiencing such a conscience if they come to the Son of God (see above John 8:36). The opposite is true in the life of a sinner. God's Word says, "The wicked flee when no man pursueth: but the righteous are bold as a lion" (Proverbs 28:1).

I will remember, as a young person, an illustration our pastor used. He said a farmer made a pledge to the church and said he would pay it in February when he sold his calf. Evidently, much time passed and the pledge was still not paid. One morning he was late arriving at church. As he came near the church, he heard them singing,

> "The half has never yet been told
> Of the blood it cleanseth me."

His conscience came alive and this farmer thought they were singing,

> "The calf has never yet been sold
> That was promised last February."

Yes, as already quoted, "The wicked flee when no man pursueth: but the righteous are bold as a lion" (Proverbs 28:1).

If you are suffering from guilt, Jesus is waiting to set you free and give you a new start. "All that the Father giveth me shall come to me; and him that cometh to me I will in no wise cast out" (John 6:37).

12
Homesick for Heaven

"For to me to live is Christ, and to die is gain. But if I live in the flesh, this is the fruit of my labour: yet what I shall choose I wot not. For I am in a strait betwixt two, having a desire to depart, and to be with Christ; which is far better: Nevertheless to abide in the flesh is more needful for you. And having this confidence, I know that I shall abide and continue with you all for your furtherance and joy of faith; That your rejoicing may be more abundant in Jesus Christ for me by my coming to you again" (Phillipians 1:21-26)

From human standards, St. Paul experienced a life of suffering (see II Corinthians 11:23-33). Jesus made it plain to would-be disciples the cost involved if they were to follow him. The Apostle Paul was no exception, for when Jesus called him out of his darkness, our Saviour said, "For I will shew him how great things he must suffer for my name's sake" (Acts 9:16).

Being human, it was only natural for the apostle to

become homesick for his eternal home when the pressure of this life weighed heavily on his soul. On one such occasion he wrote, "For we would not, brethren, have you ignorant of our trouble which came to us in Asia, that we were pressed out of measure, above strength, insomuch that we despaired even of life" (II Corinthians 1:8). When Queen Jezebel threatened the life of Elijah, the prophet "requested for himself that he might die; and said, It is enough; now, O Lord, take away my life; for I am not better than my fathers" (I Kings 19:4b).

Here we find two of God's saints, who truly loved God with all their hearts, looking for their eternal inheritance, being at home with their Lord. They were not cowards, but being human, they felt the pressures of this world. Even Jesus, by taking on himself human nature, prayed to be delivered from the cross, but never once rebelled against God's will. In Matthew 26:38-39 we read, "Then saith he unto them, My soul is exceeding sorrowful, even unto death: tarry ye here, and watch with me. And he went a little further, and fell on his face, and prayed, saying, O my Father, if it be possible, let this cup pass from me: nevertheless not as I will, but as thou wilt."

The Apostle Paul followed in the footsteps of his Master while desiring to depart and be with Jesus, yet was willing to continue his ministry in order to meet the spiritual needs of the people. He writes about being in a strait as to die and be with Christ, or to stay in this world and minister to the needs of the people.

Dr. Adam Clarke comments,

> "It appears to be a metaphor taken from the commander of a vessel, in a foreign port, who feels a strong desire... to set sail, and get to his own country and family; but this desire is counterbalanced by a conviction that the general interests of the voyage may be answered by his longer stay in the port where his vessel now rides... It would certainly be gain to

myself to die, but it will be a gain to you if I live." (*Commentary on the Bible* by Adam Clarke, "Philippians 1:23, 24." Schmul Publishing Co., 2019, vol. V.)

Years ago, we had a pastor on our district who said he had loved ones in heaven and loved ones on earth. Then he said he didn't know where he wanted to be. He was a good man and I feel sure that, like Jesus, he would want to be in the center of God's will.

I close these thoughts concerning heaven with words of encouragement from the book of Hebrews 12:1:13. Please read all thirteen verses. Verse 1 reads, "Wherefore seeing we also are compassed about with so great a cloud of witnesses, let us lay aside every weight, and the sin which doth so easily beset us, and let us run with patience the race that is set before us." The author refers us to chapter 11 which gives us a lengthy list of men and women who did great exploits for the Kingdom of God by faith. We are told that we are compassed about with these saints. It appears they are cheering us on in our race to heaven. They heard the "well done," so may we. In the Olympics, the athletes were helped by knowing the great men of the nations were watching them. The writer used this allusion to let us know we are compassed about with some of the greatest saints of the Bible. It may well be that our loved ones who died in the faith are closer to us than we think.

I had the privilege some years ago of visiting the Holy Land. I understand there were a brother and sister who sponsored these trips. One was in our country to send us, and the other was in Israel to welcome us. It was goodbye here, but good morning over there. So it will be for those who love the Lord and leave this world to be with Jesus and those who outstripped us in the race.

To some extent I can identify with the feelings of Paul

and Elijah. God willing, I may write more about the severe storms I am passing through, but God never fails. "Therefore, my beloved brethren, be ye stedfast, unmoveable, always abounding in the work of the Lord, forasmuch as ye know that your labour is not in vain in the Lord" (I Corinthians 15:58).

13
Prepared for the Storm

"Whosoever cometh to me, and heareth my sayings, and doeth them, I will shew you to whom he is like: He is like a man which built an house, and digged deep, and laid the foundation on a rock: and when the flood arose, the stream beat vehemently upon that house, and could not shake it: for it was founded upon a rock. But he that heareth, and doeth not, is like a man that without a foundation built an house upon the earth; against which the stream did beat vehemently, and immediately it fell; and the ruin of that house was great" (Luke 6:47-49).

THE ACCOUNT AS RECORDED in the Gospel of Matthew is preceded by our Saviour's Sermon on the Mount. So here in Luke, when Jesus said, "Whosoever cometh to me, and heareth my sayings, and doeth them, I will shew you to whom he is like" (Luke 6:47), he is referring not only to what he was preaching on that particular day, but all of the inspired Word of God.

In this world we share many of the problems and suffering that is the lot of both sinner and saint. Although not isolated from the storms, God promises strength for the day, and deliverance for his people. In contrast the Master spoke of the foolish man building a house without a foundation on the sand, and immediately it fell.

There's a good illustration of this truth as there were fishermen who took advantage of the dry season. The river was dry, so these men would build their huts on the sand of the river. Then, as it so often happens in the area where this took place, the rain came suddenly. The water came from the mountains in torrents. The next morning, multitudes of these huts built on the sand could not be found.

The Gospel is good news. Simply stated, God has made provision by the sacrificial death of his son, Jesus Christ, that we can be forgiven and cleansed from all sin, stand all the storms and stress of this life, because we built a firm foundation on the Rock, which is Jesus Christ.

I feel led to give my personal testimony. It was about 88 or 89 years ago that God, for Christ's sake, saved me and at age 13 sanctified me wholly. I thank God for his patience and mercy extended to me through all these years. In Isaiah 46:4 we read, "And even to your old age I am he; and even to hoar [gray, white] hairs will I carry you: I have made, and I will bear; even I will carry, and will deliver you."

God has delivered me through many storms over a period of many years. This last year has been no exception; God is still on his throne and precious to me. My wife, who encouraged and helped me in writing and many other ways, is now in a nursing home. Another brother of mine has gone to be with the Lord. My great-grandson, age 24, was attacked and lost his life.

You, reader, may be going through difficult times. Here is a promise for you: "When thou passest through the waters, I will be with thee; and through the rivers, they shall not overflow thee: when thou walkest through the fire, thou shalt not be burned; neither shall the flame kindle upon thee. For I am the Lord thy God, the Holy One of Israel, thy Saviour" (Isaiah 43:2-3a).

It has been said that someone found help in the words, "And it came to pass." Although taken out of context, it is still true according to Psalm 34:19, "Many are the afflictions of the righteous: but the Lord delivereth him out of them all."

14
A Shortcut to Certainty

"Jesus answered and said unto her, Whosoever drinketh of this water shall thirst again: But whosoever drinketh of the water that I shall give him shall never thirst; but the water that I shall give him shall be in him a well of water springing up into everlasting life. The woman saith unto him, Sir, give me this water, that I thirst not, neither come hither to draw. Jesus saith unto her, Go, call thy husband, and come hither. The woman answered and said, I have no husband. Jesus said unto her, Thou hast well said, I have no husband: For thou hast had five husbands; and he whom thou now hast is not thy husband: in that saidst thou truly. The woman saith unto him, Sir, I perceive that thou art a prophet" (John 4:13-19).

"And many of the Samaritans of that city believed on him for the saying of the woman, which testified, He told me all that ever I did" (John 4:39).

"And many more believed because of his own word;

And said unto the woman, Now we believe, not because of thy saying: for we have heard him ourselves, and know that this is indeed the Christ, the Saviour of the world" (John 4:41-42).

THE TITLE TO THIS CHAPTER may be misleading to some, causing them to think that they will arrive at certainty by their own efforts, only it will take longer. All self-effort and struggle will end in discouragement and defeat, for Jesus said, "He that entereth not by the door into the sheepfold, but climbeth up some other way, the same is a thief and a robber" (John 10:1b).

In this Samaritan village Jesus found a people ripe for the message our Saviour proclaimed. They were humble, teachable people and ready to receive Christ as a little child. Jesus says, "Whosoever shall not receive the kingdom of God as a little child, he shall not enter therein" (Mark 10:15b). The account of this revival is proof of the simple childlike faith of these people. In many other places, among more enlightened people, it was necessary for Jesus to perform miracles in order for people to believe; even so, there were those who still did not believe. Jesus raised Lazarus from the dead, and men consulted about putting Lazarus to death.

These Samaritans simply took God as faithful, and asked for no attesting miracle. Many believed in Christ, because of the testimony of the woman (see verse 39). There we come to the heritage and certainty that all may possess in Jesus Christ and be filled with the Holy Spirit. Listen to the testimony of these humble Samaritans: "And many more believed because of his own word; And said unto the woman, Now we believe, not because of thy saying: for we have heard him ourselves, and know that this is indeed the Christ, the Saviour of the world" (John 4:41-42).

After Jesus preached the Sermon on the Mount, we read, "the people were astonished at his doctrine: For he taught them as one having authority, and not as the scribes" (Matthew 7:28b-29).

The crowds learned the words of Christ expounded in a manner that was foreign to the teaching of the scribes. The message Jesus delivered was with power, certainty and left no room for Doubt.

Can we on earth be sure of our status as Christians? Can we be sure of heaven when our faith is seriously tested? I Peter 1:6b states, "in heaviness through manifold temptations." We go to God's Word for answers.

In II Corinthians 1:22 we read, "Who hath also sealed us, and given the earnest of the Spirit in our hearts." This earnest was a pledge given when purchasing property, until the final transaction took place. If you were buying a farm in those days, you would receive a container with some of the soil from the farm, thus proving you would eventually possess all the property. In Romans 8:16 Paul mentions the same truth, "The Spirit Himself beareth witness with our spirit, that we are the children of God."

Final proof of certainty comes when we can say with the Samaritans, "Now we believe, not because of thy saying: for we have heard him ourselves, and know that this is indeed the Christ, the Saviour of the world" (John 4:42b).

Years ago, in a church I pastored, a teenage girl gave a testimony I will never forget. She must have been depending on her parents' experience, for she said she now no longer depended on their experience, but she knew for herself.

What I wrote is true for this founded on the Word of God and Christian experience, but it does not mean that our faith will never be tested. I heard a chaplain who served in World War II say he noticed that after an attack there would be a counterattack. This surely happens in spiritual warfare. It was after the baptism of Jesus when he heard "a voice from heaven, saying, This is my beloved Son, in whom I am well pleased" (Matthew 3:17b). The very next verse reads, "Then was Jesus led up of the Spirit into the wilderness to be tempted of the devil" (Matthew 4:1).

This will take place in our walk with Christ. There will be times when feeling fades. At such times, we should be honest and ask our Lord if there is any spiritual cause, and take care of it if God reveals such. But there are many reasons for finding times when feeling is absent. Elijah, David, Paul, and I am sure, many others have experienced these times. Even Jesus as he faced the cross said, "My soul is exceeding sorrowful, even unto death: tarry ye here, and watch with me" (Matthew 26:38b). Sometimes, like Elijah, all we need is rest and food.

We must remember, "The just shall live by faith" (Romans 1:17b). When we walk through the valleys, remember what God showed you on the mount and you will come through victoriously. I heard a Methodist minister say the Wise Men, while following the star, had cloudy days that prevented them from seeing the star, but they followed the general direction. Likewise, we should follow the example of the Wise Men in our journey to heaven.

15
"Draw Water Out of the Wells of Salvation"
(Isaiah 12:3b)

"And I, brethren, could not speak unto you as unto spiritual, but as unto carnal, even as unto babes in Christ. I have fed you with milk, and not with meat: for hitherto ye were not able to bear it, neither yet now are ye able" (I Corinthians 3:1-2)

GOD'S PURPOSE IN CREATING man was in order to have fellowship with him. After he brought forth the lower forms of life and "saw that it was good," our Lord wanted those he could commune with on a spiritual basis and become his friends. "So God created man in his own image, in the image of God created he him; male and female created he them" (Genesis 1:27). So close is this relationship that the Apostle Paul writes, "But he that is joined unto the Lord is one spirit" (I Corinthians 6:17). In this scripture reference, the inspired writer resorts to using the analogy of the physical union between male and female, in order not only to correct the moral condition that existed in the Corinthian Church, but also that as born again and Spirit-filled Christians we are invited to enter into the very presence of the God of the universe and experience a foretaste of heaven.

From what one observes in our public worship, it appears that most praying consists in prayers of petition. It takes time to draw close to God and wait quietly before him. King David testifies, "Wait on the Lord: be of good courage, and he shall strengthen thine heart: wait, I say, on the Lord" (Psalm 27:14). In Isaiah 40:31 we read, "But they that wait upon the Lord shall renew their strength; they shall mount up with wings as eagles; they shall run, and not be weary; and they shall walk, and not faint." I realize there are times when we are not able to have our devotions as usual. At such times we can still commit our souls to God, but that should be the exception and not the rule.

The church at Corinth was not weaned from their milk diet. Paul had fed them with milk and not meat. At this writing they were still on an infant diet. There comes a time in our spiritual development that God expects us to feed ourselves. Years ago, I saw a grown animal, no longer a calf, getting its milk diet from its mother. That adult should be out grazing for itself and not dependent on the mother cow. But in the spiritual realm there are people saying, "I am not being fed by my preacher, etc." That may or may not be true. However, by the authority of God's Word, and by my experience, I testify that one can go directly to God and be fed. When we are absolutely unable to attend public worship, God can keep us. When God's people were held captive in a foreign country, we read in Ezekiel 11:16, "Therefore say, Thus saith the Lord God; Although I have cast them far off among the heathen, and although I have scattered them among the countries, yet will I be to them as a little sanctuary in the countries where they shall come."

My good wife, who has been such a help to me, is now in a nursing home, greatly afflicted and unable to walk. Although she is not able to go to her church, she is still kept by the power of almighty God. Today is Sunday, May 26th, 2019. In April I had major surgery, then went to a nursing home, and am now alone in our apartment unable to attend our church. Last December, my great-grandson was attacked and died a tragic death.

Why am I reporting my experience? It may encourage some readers to stay true who are suffering and Satan is tempting, such as he did Job, to give up the fight. Stay true. God is still in control. I have found there are seasons of relief and comfort in the midst of the storm. Personally, I have no thoughts of retreat. I am yoked to Jesus Christ, and his yoke is easy and his burden is light (see Matthew 11:28-30). In the center of a hurricane it is peaceful. So it is when the storms of life come to God's children. I remember during World War II, while preparing for the ministry at Olivet Nazarene College in Illinois, the district superintendent of Chicago Central, Dr. E.O. Chalfant, received word that his son, a paratrooper, was missing in action. The college pastor was with him. I cannot remember the exact testimony, but Dr. Chalfant told how his heart was holding steady although his head was perplexing him.

Remember you are invited to go directly to God for all your needs. "Casting all your care upon him; for he careth for you" (I Peter 5:7). "Many are the afflictions of the righteous: but the Lord delivereth him out of them all" (Psalm 34:19).

16
Contentment

"Not that I speak in respect of want: for I have learned, in whatsoever state I am, therewith to be content. I know both how to be abased, and I know how to abound: every where and in all things I am instructed both to be full and to be hungry, both to abound and to suffer need. I can do all things through Christ which strengtheneth me" (Phillipians 4:11-13).

THESE ARE THE INSPIRED WORDS of the Apostle Paul. Evidently, even this great man of God had to be trained in the school of suffering in order to understand genuine contentment. Earlier in this same epistle, he writes, "I have suffered the loss of all things, and do count them but dung, that I may win Christ" (Phillipians 3:8b). Then in the second Corinthian letter he enumerates the suffering in detail (see II Corinthians 11:23-33). Paul concluded, as we all do sooner or later, that contentment is not dependent on the circumstances of life. Then he admonishes young Timothy, "But godliness with contentment is great gain. For we brought nothing into this world, and it is certain we can carry nothing out. And having food and raiment let us be therewith content" (I Timothy 6:6-8).

In our modern day the teaching is the same, although our needs may increase in order to keep pace in the world today. The bottom line, or truth, is to be content with having our basic needs met.

I pause to give my personal testimony as to how suffering taught me a lasting lesson in contentment. At the age of 24 I was diagnosed with moderately advanced tuberculosis and suffered much for about two years, being confined in bed most of the time.

I learned to enjoy the free things of life such as fresh air and sunshine which I formerly took for granted. From my study I see beautiful trees, green grass and little birds getting their food from God. A few days ago I was sitting on the deck when a visiting squirrel came close to me. I still enjoy the many free blessings God gives us. The fact is when God fills us with his Spirit we are satisfied, and without God we will never be satisfied even if we own the entire world.

How glad and happy we should be with all the blessings God has provided. I think of the many healthy young people who are putting tattoos on their bodies, which is contrary to the Word of God. We read in Leviticus 19:28, "Ye shall not make any cuttings in your flesh for the dead, nor print any marks upon you: I am the Lord." A young man, who had an immoral tattoo on his body, came to a church I served. After his conversion, the problem of the tattoo remained. I love this family and I only write this as a warning to those who are considering tattoos. We should be content with our physical being. In our first pastorate it was necessary for my wife to be employed in order to meet our basic needs. She told me how women would come to work who had surgery on their noses, evidently thinking it would make them beautiful. We should be thankful for a healthy body.

In conclusion, and on the authority of God's Word, I say there is no lasting beauty or contentment until we put our undivided trust in our Lord Jesus Christ. "Favour is deceitful, and beauty is vain: but a woman that feareth the Lord, she shall be praised" (Proverbs 31:30).

Physical beauty soon fades. Even Jesus in his humiliation consented to come to this world without physical beauty that he might become all things to all men. We read, "...he hath no form nor comeliness; and when we shall see him, there is no beauty that we should desire him" (Isaiah 53:2b).

I write these accounts to encourage the reader to be content with the plan God in his providence has for you as an individual. "[F]or I have learned, in whatsoever state I am, therewith to be content" (Phillipians 4:11b).

17
Faithfulness as God Views It

"And he said also unto his disciples, There was a certain rich man, which had a steward; and the same was accused unto him that he had wasted his goods. And he called him, and said unto him, How is it that I hear this of thee? give an account of thy stewardship; for thou mayest be no longer steward.

"Then the steward said within himself, What shall I do? for my lord taketh away from me the stewardship: I cannot dig; to beg I am ashamed. I am resolved what to do, that, when I am put out of the stewardship, they may receive me into their houses.

"So he called every one of his lord's debtors unto him, and said unto the first, How much owest thou unto my lord? And he said, An hundred measures of oil. And he said unto him, Take thy bill, and sit down quickly, and write fifty. Then said he to another, And how much owest thou? And he said, An hundred measures of wheat. And he said unto him, Take thy bill, and write fourscore. And the lord commended the unjust steward, because he had done wisely: for the children of this world are in their generation wiser than the children of light.

"And I say unto you, Make to yourselves friends of the mammon of unrighteousness; that, when ye fail, they may receive you into everlasting habitations. He that is faithful in that which is least is faithful also in much: and he that is unjust in the least is unjust also in much. If therefore ye have not been faithful in the unrighteous mammon, who will commit to your trust the true riches? And if ye have not been faithful in that which is another man's, who shall give you that which is your own?

"No servant can serve two masters: for either he will hate the one, and love the other; or else he will hold to the one, and despise the other. Ye cannot serve God and mammon" (Luke 16:1-13).

NOTE ESPECIALLY: "He that is faithful in that which is least is faithful also in much" (Luke 16:10a).

Jesus was teaching his disciples a lesson on stewardship, using the account of a steward who was accused of wasting his employer's goods. This steward acted shrewdly in order to guarantee his future well-being in this present world. Our Lord was not condoning his action, but pointing out the steward's wisdom in attaining his livelihood while on earth. Then Jesus in verse 8 said, "And the lord commended the unjust steward, because he had done wisely: for the children of this world are in their generation wiser than the children of light."

Then, the Master clinches this message on stewardship by saying, "And I say unto you, Make to yourselves friends of the mammon of unrighteousness; that, when ye fail, they may receive you into everlasting habitations" (Luke 16:9). The word "fail" means *when we die*. If we know our Lord, converted and filled with his Holy Spirit, and continue to be faithful as good stewards of what God has blessed us with, one can only imagine our welcome to heaven. No doubt angels will welcome us. In verse 9 we read, "they may receive you." The context refers to the "mammon of unrighteousness," letting us know there will be souls in heaven because we used our money and other talents, etc., as good stewards while on earth. These redeemed saints will welcome us, saying, "I am here in heaven because you are a good steward." Yes, Sister Allen, no doubt you have already been greeted by those who made it to heaven, because years ago you saved that money to buy a coat, but a plea was made for missions and you surrendered the money you had saved even for a necessary coat.

But some will say, "I have nothing to offer." Ask God what he would have you do. The fact we are still in this world tells us our mission is not yet completed. As a boy, I passed out tracts. For many years I pastored churches. Now, my wife is in a nursing home and my health has failed in various ways, but I still have ways to serve the Lord. Above all, I can pray. God continues to bless the books I write. Some time ago, I made a list of things I could do in order to advance the Kingdom of God in my retirement.

Remember, God is interested in the quality of our work, and grades us on our faithfulness rather than our accomplishments. "He that is faithful in that which is least is faithful also in much" (Luke 16:10a).

"His lord said unto him, Well done, good and faithful servant; thou hast been faithful over a few things, I will make thee ruler over many things: enter thou into the joy of thy lord" (Matthew 25:23).

18
A Twofold Blessing

"When thou makest a dinner or a supper, call not thy friends, nor thy brethren, neither thy kinsmen, nor thy rich neighbours; lest they also bid thee again, and a recompence be made thee. But when thou makest a feast, call the poor, the maimed, the lame, the blind: And thou shalt be blessed; for they cannot recompense thee: for thou shalt be recompensed at the resurrection of the just" (Luke 14:12b-14).

THERE ARE CERTAIN fixed laws, both material and spiritual, that operate in the universe and that are irresistible. One such spiritual law is that God blesses his children more as donors than as recipients. Jesus emphatically states this truth as recorded in Acts 20:35b, "It is more blessed to give than to receive." The Holy Spirit revealed this truth to the Old Testament Prophet Isaiah. We read, "Is not this the fast that I have chosen? to loose the bands of wickedness, to undo the heavy burdens, and to let the oppressed go free, and that ye break every yoke? Is it not to deal thy bread to the hungry, and that thou bring the poor that are cast out to thy house? when thou seest the naked, that thou cover him; and that thou hide not thyself from thine own flesh? Then shall thy light break forth as the morning, and thine health shall spring forth speedily: and thy righteousness shall go before thee; the glory of the Lord shall be thy reward. Then shalt thou call, and the Lord shall answer; thou shalt cry, and he shall say, Here I am. If thou take away from the midst of thee the yoke, the putting forth of the finger, and speaking vanity; And if thou draw out thy soul to the hungry, and satisfy the afflicted soul; then shall thy light rise in obscurity, and thy darkness be as the noon day: And the Lord shall guide thee continually, and satisfy thy soul in drought, and make fat thy bones: and thou shalt be like a watered garden, and like a spring of water, whose waters fail not" (Isaiah 58:6-11).

We are not saved by our good works, but we cannot ignore the plain truth found in Titus 3:8a, "This is a faithful saying, and these things I will that thou affirm constantly, that they which have believed in God might be careful to maintain good works." We cannot remain saved without good works.

In this scripture, God is calling his people back from a religious experience which had deteriorated to outward ceremonies, such as fasting, without regards for the true practical spiritual meaning. It is a call to repentance that their joy and well-being may be restored. Isaiah outlines the sins of omission to be repented of with a promise of restoration.

I feel led to digress a bit in order to encourage those of us who love the Lord with all our heart, but are in bondage as a result of an uninstructed conscience. One of the results of being filled with the Holy Spirit is a sensitive conscience. If Satan sees that an individual will not yield to temptation, he will change his tactics and approach in a more subtle manner. In II Corinthians 2:11 we read, "Lest Satan should get an advantage of us: for we are not ignorant of his devices." We should be thankful for a sensitive conscience, but Satan can accuse us of sin by condemning us for imaginary transgressions which have no moral value. I know of a man who thought he should not smile; another good man who held a very important position as a minister in a public position, but thought he should kneel on a public sidewalk and pray. I'm not saying he did wrong, for he may have been in God's will. This good man committed suicide. I feel he became mentally unstable and was no longer capable of deciding good and evil, thus making heaven as a little innocent child. Still I know of a man who tried to walk on water and nearly drowned. The Bible tells us we are not to tempt God (see Matthew 4:5-7).

The enemy may not use such extreme measures on most of us, but if he can sidetrack us until we become self-centered, taking our "spiritual pulse" when we know all is well, we will lose much of our joy and waste precious moments that could be used in building God's Kingdom. There is a time to take spiritual inventory, even as David prayed, "Search me, O God, and know my heart: try me, and know my thoughts: And see if there be any wicked way in me, and lead me in the way everlasting" (Psalm 139:23-24).

Again, I am writing now to good God-fearing saints who too long have been held in bondage. Job is an example of one who suffered much, but found deliverance when he prayed for others. In Job 42:10 we read, "And the Lord turned the captivity of Job, when he prayed for his friends: also the Lord gave Job twice as much as he had before."

My good mother mentored me as a boy and taught me much. She lived to be almost 99 and continued to counsel me in my adult life. Now, at my advanced age, I still appreciate her insight.

Although I had already worked many years helping others, my mother noticed I still carried over a weakness of searching my own heart too much. She kindly but definitely told me that what I needed to do was to get my mind off of myself and onto others. I thought that was such true and good advice that I still have it on my "do list" at this present day. Is that what the Prophet Isaiah is saying? Read it again. Also remember what Jesus said about inviting to your meal those who are handicapped and unable to return the favor. Here is where we as a church fail. Often awards are given on the basis of achievement rather than faithfulness. Wouldn't it be good to provide a meal for the poor who really sacrificed for a worthy project? Jesus watched the giving of the people. The poor widow gave the most. The rich could give and not miss it, but she went out in her poverty, trusting Jesus to supply her need.

This chapter is titled "A Twofold Blessing" because both the recipient and donor will be blessed as these directions are put into practice.

19
A Wardrobe Change

Scripture reading: Ephesians 4:17-24 and Matthew 22:1-14

"That ye put off concerning the former conversation the old man, which is corrupt according to the deceitful lusts; And be renewed in the spirit of your mind; And that ye put on the new man, which after God is created in righteousness and true holiness" (Ephesians 4:22-24).

"And when the king came in to see the guests, he saw there a man which had not on a wedding garment: And he saith unto him, Friend, how camest thou in hither not having a wedding garment? And he was speechless. Then said the king to the servants, Bind him hand and foot, and take him away, and cast him into outer darkness, there shall be weeping and gnashing of teeth" (Matthew 22:11-13).

THE WEDDING GARMENT Jesus referred to in this parable was a long white robe provided free of charge to all who are invited as guests to the wedding festival. This garment represents the necessity of holiness in order to stand pure, clean and holy in God's presence, both now and on the Day of Judgment. "But as he which hath called you is holy, so be ye holy in all manner of conversation; Because it is written, Be ye holy; for I am holy" (I Peter 1:15-16).

What made this breach of etiquette without excuse was the fact that the robe was provided free of charge, but the guest willfully neglected that which was his responsibility. In I John 1:7 we read, "But if we walk in the light, as he is in the light, we have fellowship one with another, and the blood of Jesus Christ his Son cleanseth us from all sin." I well remember how at the age of seven or eight years of age I was definitely converted, enjoying serving the Lord, but at the age of thirteen, the Holy Spirit showed me my need of being sanctified wholly. I knelt on the bathtub and prayed, giving my all to God. I did my part, and though I had no emotion, I fully believed God, and the experience was a settling experience. What about the emotion? It came later. We should never seek emotion as such, for emotion is a by-product of a deeper experience.

But before the Holy Spirit fills our hearts, we must put off the old life of sin. I fear too many seek Jesus Christ just as an addition to the old life of sin. The prophet Balaam is an example of this truth, for he tried to hold onto two worlds and lost them both, unless he repented, but there is nowhere in God's Word that we find he ever repented.

We are not downgrading what takes place when one is saved. We are forgiven from all the sins we willfully committed, but there remains the carnal nature inherited by the fall of Adam.

So the first step in seeking to be filled with the Holy Spirit is to make sure we are saved from all our committed sins, for the Holy Spirit cannot enter a sinner's heart.

In the earlier days we kept our vegetables and fruits

by canning. Some of the jars failed to seal, causing a deadly mold. In order to reuse the jars, it was necessary to wash and boil them. Then they were fit to be refilled. So God the Holy Spirit will only enter those saved from the contagion of this world of sin.

Years ago, the writer preached a message from the scripture quoted in this writing concerning putting off the old man and putting on the new man. I illustrated it by wearing an old worn suit coat and tried to make my appearance repulsive. In the midst of my message, I took off the old coat and reached for my good suit coat, which was out of sight to the congregation. When I put on the good suit coat, the truth of this scripture was powerfully demonstrated.

We see the necessity of this experience as we study the scriptures. In his prayer for his disciples, Jesus mentions how they all are saved except the "son of perdition" (see John 17:12). Then in John 17:16-17, "They are not of the world, even as I am not of the world. Sanctify them through thy truth: thy word is truth."

Then in verse 19 Jesus prayed, "And for their sakes I sanctify myself, that they also might be sanctified through the truth."

The word "sanctify" has two meanings, one of which is *to set apart* as used many times in the Old Testament. The other is as an experience as found in I Thessalonians 5:23-24, "And the very God of peace sanctify you wholly; and I pray God your whole spirit and soul and body be preserved blameless unto the coming of our Lord Jesus Christ. Faithful is he that calleth you, who also will do it."

In verse 19 Jesus says, "I sanctify myself." Why? Jesus didn't need to seek to be sanctified wholly, but used the word in the sense of being set apart in order to make provision that his disciples might be filled with the Holy Spirit. In the second sense, the word is used as an experience. In this way we find it used in Hebrews 13:12, "Wherefore Jesus also, that he might sanctify the people with his own blood, suffered without the gate."

Last words are very important. The last words of Jesus to his followers who loved him were, "And, being assembled together with them, commanded them that they should not depart from Jerusalem, but wait for the promise of the Father, which, saith he, ye have heard of me. For John truly baptized with water; but ye shall be baptized with the Holy Ghost not many days hence" (Acts 1:4-5).

Let us all make sure we are properly attired with the wedding garment of holiness.

"Follow peace with all men, and holiness, without which no man shall see the Lord" (Hebrews 12:14).

20
"One Thing I Know"

Scripture: John 9:1-34

"Then again called they the man that was blind, and said unto him, Give God the praise: we know that this man is a sinner. He answered and said, Whether he be a sinner or no, I know not: one thing I know, that, whereas I was blind, now I see" (John 9:24-25).

THE TITLE OF THIS chapter is just four words taken from a new convert. Here we find a man born blind with no knowledge of the Word of God, but walking in what light he had. His accusers, the Pharisees, were well versed in the scriptures but unwilling to follow the clear teaching they possessed. Consequently, they not only alienated themselves from the free gift of salvation, but did their best to cause this newly converted former blind man to lose faith in Christ. The Pharisees told him that Jesus was a sinner. The new Christian said, "[O]ne thing I know, that, whereas I was blind, now I see" (John 9:25b). After he gave further testimony, the Pharisees cast him out, but Jesus found him and explained the way more clearly to him. As a result, we read, "Jesus heard that they had cast him out; and when he had found him, he said unto him, Dost thou believe on the Son of God? He answered and said, Who is he, Lord, that I might believe on him? And Jesus said unto him, Thou hast both seen him, and it is he that talketh with thee. And he said, Lord, I believe. And he worshipped him" (John 9:35-38).

Like the blind man in this account, the writer was ignorant as to how to pray a sinner's prayer. In fact, I can't remember what I said, being a very young boy, but under deep conviction. God knew my sincere desire to know him, and the experience was so real that when Satan, wicked spirits and fallen men attempt to challenge my faith, I have the assurance, "one thing I know."

I remember reading an illustration of a passenger on a boat who said to the captain, "I suppose you know every sandbar on this river." He answered, "That would be a waste of time. I know where the deep waters are."

That is the assurance God gives to those who truly follow him. We read, "The Spirit Himself beareth witness with our spirit, that we are the children of God" (Romans 8:16). This witness is spoken of as the "earnest of our inheritance" in Ephesians 1:14. It is our pledge or down payment while here on earth, assuring us of our eternal life in the world to come.

We are definitely living in the Last Days according to God's Word. Paul, in writing to Timothy, says, "This know also, that in the last days perilous times shall come" (II Timothy 3:1). Then the Apostle Paul describes things that will take place. In verse 7, "Ever learning, and never able to come to the knowledge of the truth." In the Old Testament, many years ago, the Holy Spirit inspired the Prophet Daniel to write about the trouble that will take place on the earth in the Last Days. One must read more in Daniel to get the full message, but Daniel also prophesied about learning in the Last Days. In Daniel 12:4b, "...even to the time of the end: many shall run to and fro, and knowledge shall be increased."

With all the emphasis today on knowledge, the Bible says, "...whether there be knowledge, it shall vanish away" (I Corinthians 13:8b). In the same verse it says, "Charity (love) never faileth." In the last verse, 13, we read of that which abides. "And now abideth faith, hope, charity, these three; but the greatest of these is charity [love]."

It only makes sense to seek that which is permanent. You may not have finished grade school or traveled out of the county where you were born, but if you have decided, like the man born blind, to follow Jesus, you are showing wisdom as God views it. You will be glad through all eternity for the one most important thing a human being can do, and that is to follow Jesus.

It is the birthright of God's children to know for certain that their spiritual eyes have been opened. We can testify with the former blind man, "One thing I know, that whereas I was blind, now I see."

21
Genuine Worship

"For the Levites left their suburbs and their possession, and came to Judah and Jerusalem: for Jeroboam
and his sons had cast them off from executing the
priest's office unto the Lord: And he ordained him
priests for the high places, and for the devils, and for
the calves which he had made. And after them out of
all the tribes of Israel such as set their hearts to seek
the Lord God of Israel came to Jerusalem, to sacrifice
unto the Lord God of their fathers" (II Chronicles
11:14-16).

"And he gathered all Judah and Benjamin, and the
strangers with them out of Ephraim and Manasseh,
and out of Simeon: for they fell to him out of Israel
in abundance, when they saw that the Lord his God
was with him" (II Chronicles 15:9).

"God is a Spirit: and they that worship him must worship him in spirit and in truth" (John 4:24).

"Give unto the Lord the glory due unto his name; worship the Lord in the beauty of holiness" (Psalm 29:2).

AFTER THE DEATH OF Solomon, his son Rehoboam was made king. Jeroboam had been in Egypt as an exile for fear of King Solomon. When Jeroboam heard that all Israel had come to Shechem to make Rehoboam king, Jeroboam returned from Egypt. Then the people called on Jeroboam as we read in II Chronicles 10:3-4, "And they sent and called him. So Jeroboam and all Israel came and spake to Rehoboam, saying, Thy father made our yoke grievous: now therefore ease thou somewhat the grievous servitude of thy father, and his heavy yoke that he put upon us, and we will serve thee."

Rehoboam answered the people, saying, "My father made your yoke heavy, but I will add thereto: my father chastised you with whips, but I will chastise you with scorpions" (II Chronicles 10:14b).

As a result of King Rehoboam's rough answer, ten tribes rebelled and made Jeroboam their king. In II Chronicles 10:17, we read, "But as for the children of Israel that dwelt in the cities of Judah, Rehoboam reigned over them." Other scripture leads one to believe that the tribe of Benjamin remained loyal to Rehoboam and Judah.

Thus the kingdom is now divided. Jeroboam, king of Israel, turned from God and made a religion of his liking. True worship was still practiced in Judah, and as a result those that were still in Israel who wanted a real experience with God flocked to Judah for genuine worship.

Why is it, when we have all kinds of helps, comfortable seating, much activity, etc., still many of our churches are declining or being closed? I feel we depend more on human activity and entertainment than on our God. What I write is not from a fault-finding, bitter attitude, but from a broken heart, even weeping as I write. I attended a church some time ago that has been and is still a great God-fearing church. In the midst of their service they took time for fun, singing a humorous song. I feel this was just a temporary breach in the life of this good church, but it may have had a lasting effect on some who had come to seek God.

We must teach our children the primary purpose of the church is to lead people to God and worship Him. Years ago I found a boy on the street who was probably about 9 or 10 years old. I invited him to the church where I was the pastor. He appeared to be interested, and in sincerity finally asked me, "What time does the show start?"

No one can mimic the anointing of the Holy Spirit.

I joined the church at age 13 under a pastor, who like Barnabas, "was a good man, and full of the Holy Ghost and of faith" (from Acts 11:24). Naturally, I took him as my mentor. This good man would praise the Lord as he preached by jumping up and down. As a very young man in my first pastorate, I tried to follow the example of my former pastor by jumping as he did. I was serious, but needed correction. God has shown me we need the anointing of the Holy Spirit, but manifest the blessing according to our personality. Tears of joy and deep love to God and man is part of the way God blesses me.

Our public worship services depend much on our faithfulness in our private and family devotions. We need to come to public worship with the spiritual preparation in order to hear from God; we can grieve the Holy Spirit by too much conversation unrelated to worship as we gather for a service. I was impressed when called on to preach for a certain church. A group of men took me aside and prayed for me before I preached.

Once we are anointed by the Holy Spirit, we must be careful to maintain that close relationship. I make it a practice to find a secret place a few minutes before I preach to be alone with God who loves me.

In order to get the attention of people, some will tell a joke that has no spiritual significance whatever, and even worse joke about spiritual things, which is one way to take the name of God in vain. One may have temporarily gained the attention of the congregation but lost the presence of God.

There is nothing that will get and hold the attention of a congregation like the coming of the Holy Spirit on our singing, testimonies, praying and preaching.

"I am the vine, ye are the branches: He that abideth in me, and I in him, the same bringeth forth much fruit: for without me ye can do nothing" (John 15:5).

22
A Subtle Danger

"Then came to Jesus scribes and Pharisees, which were of Jerusalem, saying, Why do thy disciples transgress the tradition of the elders? for they wash not their hands when they eat bread. But he answered and said unto them, Why do ye also transgress the commandment of God by your tradition? For God commanded, saying, Honour thy father and mother: and, He that curseth father or mother, let him die the death. But ye say, Whosoever shall say to his father or his mother, It is a gift, by whatsoever thou mightest be profited by me; And honour not his father or his mother, he shall be free. Thus have ye made the commandment of God of none effect by your tradition. Ye hypocrites, well did Esaias prophesy of you, saying, This people draweth nigh unto me with their mouth, and honoureth me with their lips; but their heart is far from me. But in vain they do worship me, teaching for doctrines the commandments of men" (Matthew 15:1-9).

THE SCRIBES AND Pharisees mentioned in verse one had so walked against "That… true Light, which lighteth every man that cometh into the world" (see John 1:9) until they were blinded to spiritual reality. In this depraved spiritual condition they felt it was necessary to put the final touch on the inspired Word of God. This was called the "tradition of the elders." Jesus said they taught these commandments as doctrine, although they were just commands of men.

Then our Lord gave an example of how they perverted the inspired Word of God. Jesus rebuked the scribes and Pharisees by saying how they failed to honor their parents by not supporting them. "Honour" as used here meant not only respect and submission, but also supplying their physical needs. They used the tradition by saying the gift was already dedicated for the work of God. Then, in this way they failed to honour their father and mother. By doing this they escaped the duty of providing for their parents.

But were the scribes and Pharisees the only ones guilty of this disguised sin? What about the church today? This is the sin of the ditch on one side of the straight and narrow way "which leadeth unto life" (see Matthew 7:14) while worldliness is the ditch on the other side. The sin Jesus denounces the scribes and Pharisees as committing is a subtle temptation that Satan uses against those who really love God and want to live a wholly sanctified life. I think I am correct in saying that the Pharisees in their origin were a sincere people who desired to live a holy life, but their religious experience had deteriorated until it mainly consisted of man-made rules known as the tradition of the elders. Many examples are found in the Gospels regarding how they lost their love for God and man, but were very intent on keeping their man-made rules, the tradition of the elders.

Lest I be misunderstood in what I write, I want to make it clear that I believe we should have standards as guidelines as an aid to our walk with God. This helped me avoid some sinful habits. I was reared in a very conservative holiness church and I am still very conservative as it relates to essentials.

What I am saying is no more than Jesus said. Our danger, as with the scribes and Pharisees, is when we teach these standards as doctrine instead of showing by the Word of God the sin we mention. A lady in one of my pastorates quoted the manual of our church, saying, "The manual says…" She should have quoted from the Bible.

You cannot legislate sin out of the human heart. A young man had recently become a Christian, and as far as I know must have had no knowledge of what our church had as standards. But very soon after his conversion, he told me some of the things God had shown him to be sinful. They were the same things we had in our church manual. We need to pray and give God time to work.

Years ago, when I was concerned about standards, I brought it to the attention of my district superintendent. He gave me good advice when he said, "Keep the spiritual tide high," or similar words.

If we follow the path of the scribes and Pharisees by adding to the inspired Word of God, thinking we are saved if we keep our modern "tradition of the elders," the results will finally be the same as it was with the scribes and Pharisees. One soon gets in bondage. It will be a matter of trying to keep your religious experience instead of your experience keeping you. Then the enemy will suggest more and more you must do to please God. Finding this impossible, one will lose the joy and romance of serving God and will share the feeling of Israel serving their taskmasters in Egypt. In this condition one may be tempted to become harsh, critical and even bitter. When one has lost the joy, Satan will quickly take advantage of one's condition by tempting one to give up and sin. Since "the joy of the Lord is your strength" (Nehemiah 8:10b) and you have lost the joy, you may become an easy prey for the enemy.

Reader, if you are coming near this dangerous cliff of sin, which was the downfall of the scribes and Pharisees, don't give up, just walk in new light as God leads you. "But if we walk in the light, as he is in the light, we have fellowship one with another, and the blood of Jesus Christ his Son cleanseth us from all sin" (I John 1:7). "If the Son therefore shall make you free, ye shall be free indeed" (John 8:36).

23
Forgiveness for the Vilest

"If thou, Lord, shouldest mark iniquities, O Lord, who shall stand? But there is forgiveness with thee, that thou mayest be feared" (Psalm 130:3-4).

"If we confess our sins, he is faithful and just to forgive us our sins, and to cleanse us from all unrighteousness" (I John 1:9).

"My little children, these things write I unto you, that ye sin not. And if any man sin, we have an advocate with the Father, Jesus Christ the righteous: And he is the propitiation for our sins: and not for ours only, but also for the sins of the whole world" (I John 2:1-2).

YEARS AGO, AN ARTICLE appeared in one of our periodicals with the caption, "If alcohol is a disease, let us isolate the germ!" We all know that would be impossible, since no germ is involved, but alcoholism is an acquired condition brought on oneself by his or her personal choices.

But the bottom line is that all sins stem from a sinful condition of the heart known as original sin, and every individual is born with this sin. After King David sinned so deeply, he confessed this truth in his prayer of repentance in Psalm 51:5, "Behold, I was shapen in iniquity; and in sin did my mother conceive me." David is not saying he was born out of wedlock, but he was born as we all are with a tendency to sin until God cleanses our heart from original sin. In verse seven of this song, he prays, "Purge me with hyssop, and I shall be clean: wash me, and I shall be whiter than snow." King David not only wanted his actual sins forgiven, but he wanted a deep cleansing of his heart, the cause of him going astray. Pentecost made the difference in the disciples after they were filled with the Holy Spirit in the Upper Room (see Acts 2).

Too long we have been hacking at the branches and leaving the root which will sprout new branches. We had a shrub that had roots that were inaccessible. I could have continued to cut the branches off, but I finally purchased a solution that I sprayed on the leaves and it went deep to the roots and took care of the problem.

There is much talk today about being born with a different lifestyle. Sin manifests itself in various ways but all comes from a corrupt heart. Those who follow unnatural sins of the flesh can be changed when they come to Jesus. It was for these and all sinners that Jesus Christ came to save. Some may think their sins are too hideous to be forgiven, but listen to what our dear Saviour says to such: "Wherefore I say unto you, All manner of sin and blasphemy shall be forgiven unto men: but the blasphemy against the Holy Ghost shall not be forgiven unto men" (Matthew 12:31). You have not committed blasphemy against the Holy Ghost (Holy Spirit) if you have a sincere desire to know Jesus Christ with the Holy Spirit drawing you to our dear Saviour. This is in keeping with the Word of God. "No man can come to me, except the Father which hath sent me draw him: and I will raise him up at the last day" (John 6:44). Also, John 6:37 reads, "All that the Father giveth me shall come to me; and him that cometh to me I will in no wise cast out." Satan will resist all who seek the Lord, but the Seeker must claim the promise of God and believe. "If we confess our sins, he is faithful and just to forgive us our sins, and to cleanse us from all unrighteousness" (I John 1:9).

"The Lord is not slack concerning his promise, as some men count slackness; but is longsuffering to us-ward, not willing that any should perish, but that all should come to repentance" (II Peter 3:9).

24
Spiritual Renewal

"Thou, O God, didst send a plentiful rain, whereby thou didst confirm thine inheritance, when it was weary" (Psalm 68:9).

WHILE THIS VERSE PROBABLY refers to the temporal need of the children of Israel, it is certainly true in the realm of the spiritual. The Spirit-filled servants of God will experience this renewal many times as they walk in harmony with God.

There is a tendency to become lax in serving our Saviour during what has often been called the "good times." It was so in the life of Israel. Nehemiah mentions one of these times when God's people were seemingly blessed beyond measure (see Nehemiah 9:20-25). It was at this time of manifold blessing and rest when Israel fell into sin. We read the account in Nehemiah 9:28, "But after they had rest, they did evil again before thee: therefore leftest thou them in the land of their enemies, so that they had the dominion over them: yet when they returned, and cried unto thee, thou heardest them from heaven; and many times didst thou deliver them according to thy mercies."

100 SPIRITUAL GLEANINGS FROM EVERYDAY LIFE

It appears God's people failed in those ancient times because times were so good that they no longer felt their need and dependence on God. The reverse of this strategy of Satan is the temptation to cast away our confidence when the "hard times" come and it is with difficulty we pray and seek God's face. It is during such times that the enemy may come with a severe temptation to lure us to sin by disobeying God. It was so in the life of our forerunner, Jesus Christ. We read of this in the account of our Savior's baptism, "And Jesus, when he was baptized, went up straightway out of the water: and, lo, the heavens were opened unto him, and he saw the Spirit of God descending like a dove, and lighting upon him: And lo a voice from heaven, saying, This is my beloved Son, in whom I am well pleased" (Matthew 3:16-17). Then the next verse, Matthew 4:1, says, "Then was Jesus led up of the Spirit into the wilderness to be tempted of the devil."

I am again reminded of the World War II chaplain who said that he noticed that after an attack there would be a counterattack. The same is true in our spiritual war. Numerous times I have observed this taking place when a revival is scheduled, and also in my personal experience serving the Lord.

Let us follow our Lord's example in these battles. Jesus resisted the adversary by quoting the scripture, "Thy word have I hid in mine heart, that I might not sin against thee" (Psalm 119:11).

Finally, after resisting the enemy, Jesus said, "Get thee hence, Satan: for it is written, Thou shalt worship the Lord thy God, and him only shalt thou serve" (Matthew 4:10b). "Submit yourselves therefore to God. Resist the devil, and he will flee from you" (James 4:7).

There comes a time in our testing when by the help of God, we stand by faith and see the salvation of the Lord. By all means read Ephesians 6:10-18.

When our dear Saviour resisted the enemy we read, "Then the devil leaveth him" (Matthew 4:11a). Not only did the devil leave, but "angels came and ministered unto him" (Matthew 4:11b).

Some of the sweetest times I have known have been after some of the most perplexing, difficult spiritual battles I have experienced. Never give up! In closing, I now give scripture that has and continues to help and guide me in my spiritual warfare:

> "I had fainted, unless I had believed to see the goodness of the Lord in the land of the living. Wait on the Lord: be of good courage, and he shall strengthen thine heart: wait, I say, on the Lord" (Psalm 27:13-14).

> "...in quietness and in confidence shall be your strength..." (part of Isaiah 30:15).

> "He giveth power to the faint; and to them that have no might he increaseth strength. Even the youths shall faint and be weary, and the young men shall utterly fall: But they that wait upon the Lord shall renew their strength; they shall mount up with wings as eagles; they shall run, and not be weary; and they shall walk, and not faint" (Isaiah 40:29-31).

25
Placing Our Priorities

"[T]hey made me the keeper of the vineyards; but mine own vineyard have I not kept" (Song of Solomon 1:6b).

DR. HARDY C. POWERS, a beloved late general superintendent of the Church of the Nazarene, told of an experience he had as he gave an examination to a class studying for the ministry. One of the questions asked, "What is the first duty of a general superintendent?" In answer to the question, one of the students answered, "The first duty of a general superintendent is to save his own soul." While the answer was not correct as to the government of our church, we all would agree with the student's answer.

The Bible gives many examples of those who helped others, but neglected the cultivation of their own souls. We see this tragedy taking place in our own day.

However you interpret verse 6, one truth remains, and that is, this Shulamite neglected her personal responsibility while performing the duties assigned to her as related to others. Even if taken out of context, the spiritual truth remains, which is, we can point others to Jesus Christ but neglect our own spiritual condition and finally be lost.

King Saul was chosen to serve, but failed later in life. "And Samuel said to all the people, See ye him whom the Lord hath chosen, that there is none like him among all the people?" (I Samuel 10:24a) Then in I Samuel 28:15 we read Saul's words, "I am sore distressed; for the Philistines make war against me, and God is departed from me, and answereth me no more" (part of verse 15).

As a young man, "Solomon loved the Lord" (see I Kings 3:3), but turned from God in his old age. "For it came to pass, when Solomon was old, that his wives turned away his heart after other gods: and his heart was not perfect with the Lord his God, as was the heart of David his father" (I Kings 11:4). God inspired King Solomon to write part of our Bible, but later he turned away from the true and living God he loved and served as a young man.

Even the Apostle Paul, a great saint, was watchful in caring for his own spiritual condition. He said, "But I keep under my body, and bring it into subjection: lest that by any means, when I have preached to others, I myself should be a castaway" (I Corinthians 9:27). In Hebrews 3:12-14 we read, "Take heed, brethren, lest there be in any of you an evil heart of unbelief, in departing from the living God. But exhort one another daily, while it is called To day; lest any of you be hardened through the deceitfulness of sin. For we are made partakers of Christ, if we hold the beginning of our confidence stedfast unto the end" (Hebrews 3:12-14).

Let us remember what Jesus says, "For the Son of Man is as a man taking a far journey, who left his house, and gave authority to his servants, and to every man his work, and commanded the porter to watch. Watch ye therefore: for ye know not when the master of the house cometh, at even, or at midnight, or at the cockcrowing, or in the morning: Lest coming suddenly he find you sleeping. And what I say unto you I say unto all, Watch" (Mark 13:34-37).

www.ingramcontent.com/pod-product-compliance
Lightning Source LLC
Chambersburg PA
CBHW060031050426
42448CB00012B/2960